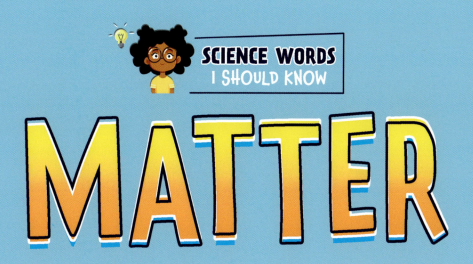

MATTER

by Alexandria Berry

Published in the United States of America by Cherry Lake Publishing Group
Ann Arbor, Michigan
www.cherrylakepublishing.com

Reading Adviser: Beth Walker Gambro, MS, Ed., Reading Consultant, Yorkville, IL

Photo Credits:
© Nicoleta Ionescu/Shutterstock, (cartoon girl on cover and throughout book), © VisualArtStudio/Shutterstock, (photo) cover; © Cassette Bleue/Shutterstock, speech bubbles throughout; © Pond Saksit/Shutterstock, (girl), © KRIACHKO OLEKSII/Shutterstock, (butterfly), © Yeti studio/Shutterstock, (ice), page 5; © LarysaPol/Shutterstock, (rocks), © DesignSpread/Shutterstock, (bear), page 6; © Prostock-studio/Shutterstock, © Bogdanovich_Alexander/Shutterstock, (rubber pencil), © Maren Winter/Shutterstock, (wood pencils), page 7; © New Africa/Shutterstock, (top), page 8; © SeventyFour/Shutterstock, page 9; © New Africa/Shutterstock, (boy), © gresei/Shutterstock, (glass), page 10; © baibaz/Shutterstock, (honey), © Sergey Novikov/Shutterstock, page 11; © SUKJAI PHOTO/Shutterstock, (painting), © Hatchapong Palurtchaivong/Shutterstock, page 12; © New Africa/Shutterstock, (top), © Vintage Tone/Shutterstock, page 13; © Roman Samborskyi/Shutterstock, (girl), © Kameel4u/Shutterstock, (kite), © Pornsawan Baipakdee/Shutterstock, (trees), page 14; © allensima/Shutterstock, page 15; © bearmoney/Shutterstock, (top), © Ulga/Shutterstock, (bottom), page 16; © Andrei Kobylko/Shutterstock, (top), © New Africa/Shutterstock, (blue balloon), page 17; © WhiteFrame Studios/Shutterstock, page 18; © Pepermpron/Shutterstock, (illustration), © kazoka/Shutterstock, page 19; © Rudy Balasko/Shutterstock, page 20; © Evgeny Atamanenko/Shutterstock, (bike), © Tiny Art/Shutterstock, page 21

Produced by bluedooreducation.com for Cherry Lake Publishing

Copyright © 2026 by Cherry Lake Publishing Group

All rights reserved. No part of this book may be reproduced or utilized in any form or by any means without written permission from the publisher.

Library of Congress Cataloging-in-Publication Data has been filed and is available at catalog.loc.gov.

Printed in the United States of America

Note from Publisher: Websites change regularly, and their future contents are outside of our control. Supervise children when conducting any recommended online searches for extended learning opportunities.

TABLE OF CONTENTS

Everything Around You 4

Solids 6

Liquids 9

Gases 13

Changes in Matter 18

Think About It 22
Glossary 23
Find Out More 24
Index 24
About the Author 24

EVERYTHING AROUND YOU

Look at the cover of this book.
What is the bubble filled with?

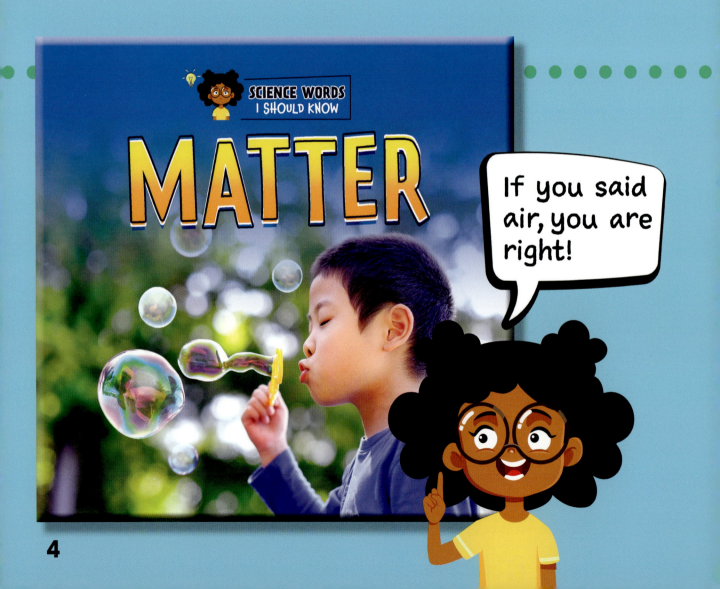

If you said air, you are right!

Air is a type of **matter**. Matter can be hard, soft, wet, or even invisible!

Everything you see is made of matter—even you!

5

SOLIDS

All matter takes up space. Some matter is **solid**. Solids can be hard, like a rock. Others are soft, like a teddy bear.

Solids keep their shape. A ball stays round. A box stays square. Solids keep their shape unless you cut or break them.

A ball will stay round unless someone pops it.

Solids Can Be Bendy or Stiff?

Yes. You can bend a pencil made of rubber. You can't bend a pencil made of wood.

7

Solids can feel very different. They can have different **textures**, such as rough or smooth.

Clay keeps its shape until you cut or press it. You can change the clay's shape, but it's still a solid.

1 Takes up space

2 Keeps its shape when left alone

2 Can be many textures

This is how you know something is a solid.

LIQUIDS

Liquids can move and flow. Water, milk, and juice are all liquids.

You can pour liquids.

A liquid takes the shape of its **container**.

10

Some liquids are thick, like honey. Others are thin, like water.

All liquids move, but some flow slower than others.

Honey is a thick liquid that flows slowly.

Liquids are important. We drink liquids like water and juice to stay healthy.

We use liquids to paint, clean, and cook.

1 Takes up space

2 Can move and flow

3 Takes the shape of its container

This is how you know something is a liquid.

GASES

Gases are all around us, even though we can't see them. They spread out to fill any space, such as a balloon or a room.

Gases make balloons grow.

The bubbles in soda are made of a gas!

13

You can't see most gases, but you can feel them. Blow on your hands and feel the air moving. Air is a gas!

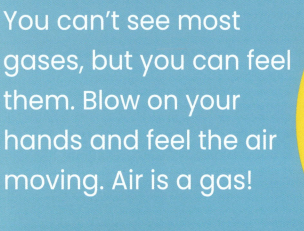

The wind is air moving all around you.

Air can move so fast that it makes trees sway and waves crash in the ocean.

Gases help us breathe. The air we breathe has an important gas called **oxygen**.

We have air inside our lungs.

Gas helps us cook. Some stoves use gas to make flames.

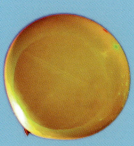

1	2	3
Spreads out to fill any space	Most cannot be seen	Doesn't have a shape

This is how you know something is a gas.

"A gas called helium makes balloons float up in the air."

Trapping a Gas

Blow up a balloon and tie it. You've trapped gas inside! Pop the balloon, and the gas escapes. The gas will spread to fill its new space.

CHANGES IN MATTER

Matter can go through different changes. Some kinds of solids **melt** when they get warm.

solid

Ice cream changes from a solid to a liquid on a warm day.

liquid

18

Water Can Be a Solid, Liquid, or Gas

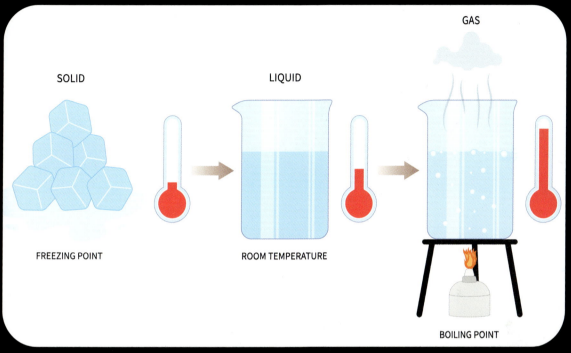

SOLID — FREEZING POINT
LIQUID — ROOM TEMPERATURE
GAS — BOILING POINT

Water becomes ice when it freezes. Ice is a solid.

Ice turns into water when it warms. Water is a liquid.

Water becomes steam when it boils. Steam is a gas.

Look for steam when you heat water to its boiling point.

gas

People build things with matter. Homes, bridges, and schools are made of strong solids like bricks and metal.

The bricks, glass, and metal in buildings are matter.

Cars, bikes, and planes are made of matter. They help us get where we need to go!

Matter is everywhere as a solid, liquid, or gas.

Keep exploring the world and see how amazing matter can be.

21

THINK ABOUT IT

What did you learn in this book? Match each sentence to the correct picture.

1 This picture shows a liquid.

2 This picture shows a gas.

3 This is a soft solid.

4 This solid is frozen water.

A.

B.

C.

D.

Answers: 1C 2D 3A 4B

22

GLOSSARY

container (kuhn-TAY-ner) an object, such as a jar or a box, that holds something

gases (GAS-iz) types of matter that don't have shape, like air, and fill any space around them

liquids (LIK-widz) types of matter that flow and take the shape of their containers

matter (MAT-ur) everything around you that is solid, liquid, or gas

melt (MELT) warming a solid until it turns into a liquid

oxygen (AHK-sih-juhn) a gas in the air that people and animals need to breathe

solid (SAH-lid) matter that has a shape, like a ball or a box

textures (TEKS-churz) the ways things feel, such as rough, smooth, soft, or hard

Find Out More

Books
Bernhardt, Caroline. *Science Starters: Light*. Minnetonka, MN: Bellwether Media, 2019

Schuh, Mari C. *Let's Look At Light: Is It Light or Dark?* Mankato, MN: Pebble Books, 2019

Websites
Search these online sources with an adult:

Matter | PBS Kids

Matter | Science Trek

Index

change(s) 8, 18
gas(es) 13, 14, 15, 16, 17, 19, 21
liquid(s) 9, 10, 11, 12, 18, 19, 21
melt 18
shape 7, 8, 10, 12, 17
solid(s) 6, 7, 8, 18, 19, 20, 21

About the Author

Alexandria Berry is a science enthusiast who loves exploring the world of matter, especially hiking in the great outdoors. As a fifth-grade teacher, she is passionate about inspiring young minds to explore the wonders of the natural world.